GW01465789

NELSON'S NEW WEST INDIAN READERS

INTRODUCTORY BOOK 1

REVISED EDITION

CLIVE BORELY

Illustrated by LYNNE WILLEY

OXFORD
UNIVERSITY PRESS

OXFORD
UNIVERSITY PRESS

Great Clarendon Street, Oxford, OX2 6DP, United Kingdom

Oxford University Press is a department of the University of Oxford.
It furthers the University's objective of excellence in research, scholarship,
and education by publishing worldwide. Oxford is a registered trade mark of
Oxford University Press in the UK and in certain other countries

Text © Clive Borely 1974, 1988
Original illustrations © Oxford University Press 2015

The moral rights of the authors have been asserted

First published by Thomas Nelson and Sons Ltd in 1974
Second edition published by Thomas Nelson and Sons Ltd in 1988
This edition published by Oxford University Press in 2015

All rights reserved. No part of this publication may be reproduced,
stored in a retrieval system, or transmitted, in any form or by any
means, without the prior permission in writing of Oxford University
Press, or as expressly permitted by law, by licence or under terms
agreed with the appropriate reprographics rights organization.
Enquiries concerning reproduction outside the scope of the above
should be sent to the Rights Department, Oxford University Press, at
the address above.

You must not circulate this work in any other form and you must
impose this same condition on any acquirer

British Library Cataloguing in Publication Data
Data available

978-0-1756-6356-9

10 9 8 7 6 5 4 3

Printed in India

Acknowledgements

Although we have made every effort to trace and contact all
copyright holders before publication this has not been possible in all
cases. If notified, the publisher will rectify any errors or omissions at
the earliest opportunity.

Links to third party websites are provided by Oxford in good faith
and for information only. Oxford disclaims any responsibility for
the materials contained in any third party website referenced in
this work.

Note to the Teacher

Introductory Books 1 and 2 constitute the second half of the **Nelson New West Indian Readers** programme intended for infant departments of primary schools. **Infant Books 1 and 2,** the first half of the programme, are based on a phonic approach to the teaching of reading to which certain elements of 'look and say' and other methods have been added. The **Introductory Books** continue this phonic approach, and you are reminded that the suggestions made in the **Infant Books** need to be continued. The **Introductory Books** do not have the appearance of phonic texts. This is because the phonic rules covered in **Infant Books 1 and 2** have made it possible to generate a wide vocabulary which can be used without the unnatural rhyming sentences which are a feature of many phonic readers.

The first three pages of **Introductory Book 1** are written to recall the characters of the **Infant Books** and give pupils a feeling of confidence in the new readers.

The new material in the **Introductory Books** takes the young reader into words of two and three syllables. The first step is taken with the introduction of the past tense form of the verb, e.g. **look – looked; like – liked,** etc. You should first revise the uninflected form of all the verbs on the page, reminding the class of the phonic rules they might have forgotten. Then you should show how '-ed' when added to these words indicates past tense. The class should then be made to read the words in pairs: **look – looked; like – liked,** etc. You should point out how, with words ending in 'y', the 'y' changes to 'i' before the '-ed' is added. The 'ow' sound as in **cow** should be introduced in the same way as was done in the **Infant Books,** along with its alternative spelling 'ou'. Children should be taught the sound 'owl' as a unit, and then combined with different initial consonants. With 'ou', they can be taught this sound and then made to pronounce the words in stages, e.g., **ou – lou – loud.** The lengthening 'e', and the 'alk' which were used in the **Infant Books** are practised here as well.

The other rules introduced in **Introductory Book 1** are 'oo' as in **pool;** 'or' as in **port,** the final 'sh' as in **hush,** and the '-er' suffix as in **run – runner, teach – teacher;** the '-al' and '-le' as in **medal** and **handle;** the '-er', '-est' suffix of the comparative and superlative (**fast, faster, fastest**) of adjectives; and the '-ist' suffix as in **cycle – cyclist.**

Introductory Book 2 aims to give further practice in dealing with words of two or more syllables and introduces a number of new 'look and say' words.

You will see that there are few new phonic rules added in the **Introductory Books**. At this stage pupils have learnt the basic rules of single syllable words. They have learnt all the consonant sounds and all the short vowel sounds, and are able to combine these to form words or syllables. They have learnt the long vowel combinations, e.g. 'ai', 'ea', 'ou', and the lengthening 'e' rule.

They have also learnt the major and final consonants, and have been introduced to the suffixes of tense and comparison.

You should now help them to develop the competence and confidence to use these rules readily and to develop the ability to 'work out' and recognise the most frequently used words automatically. This means engaging in such activities as phonic word building by the use of the blackboard or word charts, reading of phrase groups, and the making of short reading passages designed to give practice in specially selected rules for revision. Reading of the lesson in the textbook should not be viewed as the sole or even primary objective of the reading lesson. The child is not being taught **to read a book** , but **to read.** The stories serve as an incentive to the child and successful reading of them indicates a growth in reading skill, but the teacher must engage in all the preliminary and back-up activities that lead to real mastery of this important skill.

Clive Borely

Here are some of our old friends.
We met them in the last book.
This is Ann.
She likes to help her mummy cook.
She likes to bake chocolate cake with
   cherries.

Here is Dave.
He likes to play with his pets.
He also likes to ride in Mr Hoad's new boat.
When the tide is right, Mr Hoad takes Dave
    to fish with him.
This is their father.
He is a friend of Mr Hoad's.
He takes our friends for picnics on the
    beach.

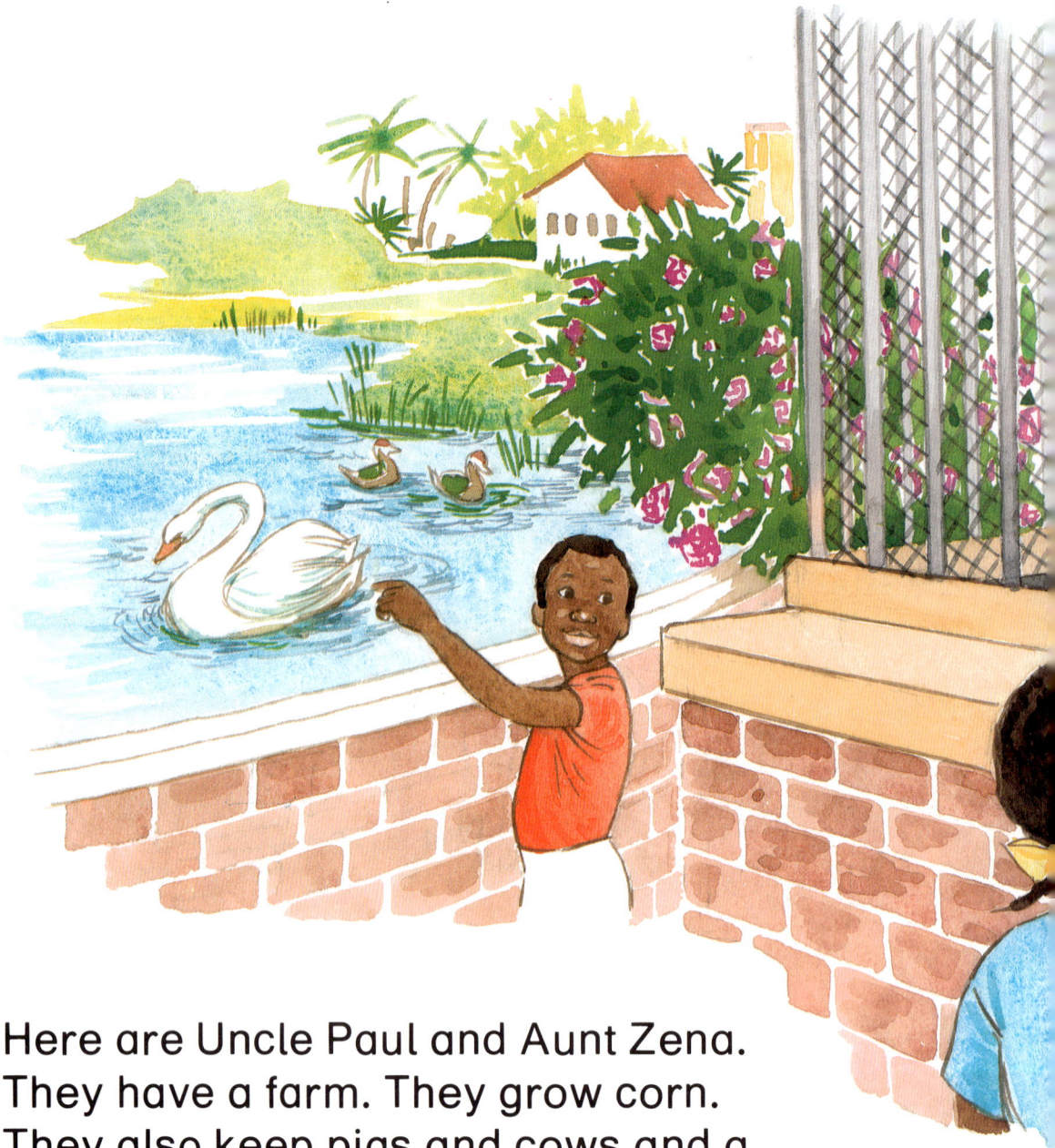

Here are Uncle Paul and Aunt Zena.
They have a farm. They grow corn.
They also keep pigs and cows and a
　　donkey.
One day the donkey made the children
　　jump with his loud "Hee haw."
Our friends spent a day at the zoo.
They gave nuts to the monkeys.
They fed the birds and threw popcorn for
　　the swan which swam in the pond.

look	looked	try	tried	cow
like	liked	cry	cried	how
pick	picked	fry	fried	now
lick	licked	dry	dried	sow
		reply	replied	brow

One day David and Tim went to see Aunt
  Zena.
"Good morning, Aunt Zena," said Tim and
  David.
"Good morning, boys," replied Aunt Zena.
"I'm so glad to see you. I hope you've
  come to help me on the farm."
"Yes," said Tim.
David did not like work.
He liked to run about and chat to the parrot.
He liked to look at the cow and the big, fat
  sow and her piglets.

"What about you, David? Will you help
    too?" asked Aunt Zena.
David looked up and said,
    "Yes, Aunt Zena, I'll help too."
"Good boy," said Aunt Zena. "Come with
    me. Uncle Paul is working at the back of
    the house. We'll ask him how you can
    help."

owl	loud	root	rule	walk
fowl	proud	boot	rude	talk
howl	cloud	tool	mule	chalk
growl	out	stool		
	shout	cool		
	stout	fool		
		pool		

Uncle Paul was in the tool shed.

"Hello boys, have you come to help me?"

"Yes, Uncle Paul," they said.

"Good. You can help me take the tools
   outside. I'm going to make a run for the
   fowls."

Uncle Paul took up the saw and a box of
   nails.

Tim took up the hammer and a rule
   and went out with Uncle Paul.

David sat on a stool in the tool shed.
He did not help carry the tools.
Then he saw a pair of boots.
They were Uncle Paul's tall boots.
They were too tall for David,
    but he didn't care. He put them on.
"Now I'll go for a walk in my boots,"
    said David, as he walked out of the shed.

Tim helped Uncle Paul dig holes.
Uncle Paul put poles into the holes.
Then Tim filled the holes with dirt.
"That's good, Tim. Thanks a lot,"
    said Uncle Paul.
Tim put the extra dirt at the root
    of the grapefruit tree.
"That's good," said Uncle Paul.
    "One day you will become a fine
    farmer."
Tim was very proud to hear that.

"Can I pick some grapefruit, Uncle Paul?"
   asked Tim.
"The grapefruits are not ripe yet. But you
   can pick some mangoes if you like," said
   Uncle Paul.
Tim ran over to the mango tree.
He climbed up the tree, and picked a
   mango and took a bite.

14

"Boy, this mango is sweet," he said.
"Get some for David and the others,"
    said Uncle Paul.
"Yes," said Tim. "They will love these
    mangoes. They are so sweet."
Just then there was a loud howl. Tim
    jumped.
"Where is David?" asked Uncle Paul.
"I left him in the tool shed," said Tim.

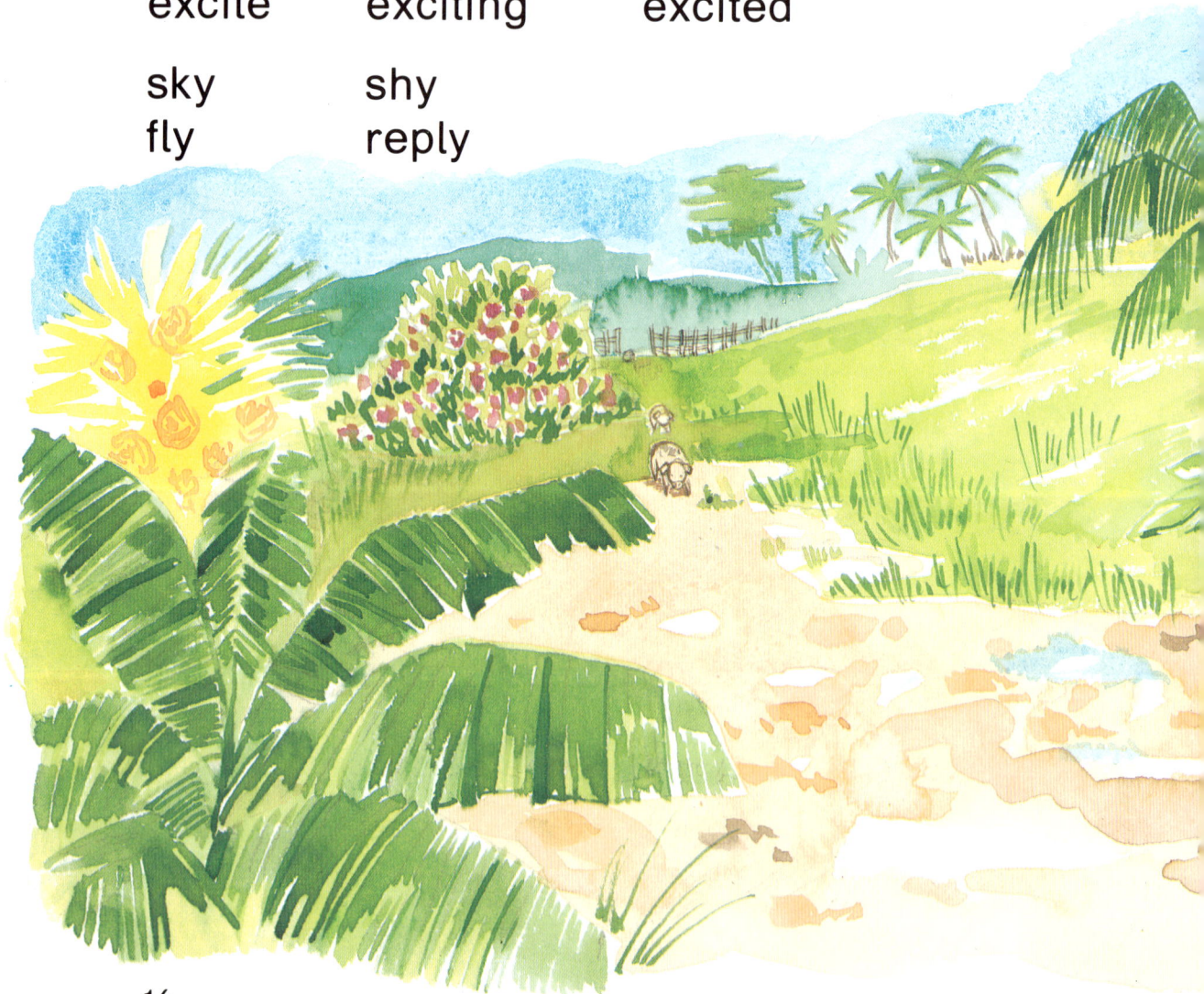

walk	walking	walked
talk	talking	talked
pick	picking	picked
wear	wearing	

want	wanting	wanted
shout	shouting	shouted
wait	waiting	waited
excite	exciting	excited

sky	shy
fly	reply

David had walked out of the tool shed.
He had put on Uncle Paul's tall boots.
"I am a big giant," he said to himself.
He made long steps in the big boots.
"I'll go and scare the others," he said.
"I'll walk up to Tim and make a loud growl.
    That will scare him."

David saw the pig with her piglets. He went
   up to them.
"Come, little piggy," he said. "Come to
   me."
David picked up a little piglet.
It cried, "Wee, wee."
The big sow was looking for her piglet.
She heard his cry. She looked and saw
   David holding it.
The big, fat sow ran to David.

David dropped the piglet and tried to run,
   but the boots were too big for him.
He could not run.
He fell on his face in a pool of mud.

The sow was still running towards him.
He howled and howled. Uncle Paul and Tim
  ran up to him. They picked him up.
"Poor little David," said Uncle Paul. "Don't
  cry."
"I don't want to be a giant any more," said
  David.

"Don't cry, Dave," said Uncle Paul.
"Those boots are too big for you. If you
want to help, I'll get a pair of small boots
for you."
"I don't like that old pig. I want to go
home," cried David.

pool	port	hush	run	runner
stool	sport	rush	teach	teacher
school	short	brush	start	starter

The girls ran home from school. Ann was
    excited.
"Mummy, we have great news.
    Our school is going to have a Sports Day.
    Can I take part?"

"Can I take part, too?" shouted Joan.

"Okay, okay," said Mother. "One at a time, please."

"What do you want to do, Ann?"

"I want to run for my class," said Ann.

"And you, Joan. What do you want?"

"I want to take part in the egg and spoon race."

Just then the boys rushed in.

"Mom," called Sam. "We are having
our Sports Day soon. I am going
to take part. I want to win every race."

"You can't win every race," said Ann.
"You are too fat to run fast."

"I can beat you in a race," shouted Sam.

"So what?" said Ann. "You're older than
me and your legs are longer.
Why don't you race Mohan?
He'll beat you by a mile."

Sam wanted to reply, but he could not.
He knew that Mohan was a very good
   runner.
He knew that he could not beat Mohan in a
   race.
"I don't care if I am fat," he replied at last.
   "I'm sure to be picked for the tug-of-war.
   I know we'll win that."

The boys and girls began to get ready
for the Sports Day. Mohan and Sita
got up early and ran around the block.
Joan and David ran races in the park.
Sam did not run.
"I don't need to run races," said Sam.
"I am going to eat to get strong
to help win the tug-of-war."

"Come Ann, let's run a race," said Joan.
"Okay," replied Ann. "Let's run from here
   to that pole."
"Yes, come Sam. You start this race."
"Okay," said Sam.
"Ready. . .steady. . .GO!"

Ann and Joan ran fast.
They ran neck and neck all the way.
Then in the end Joan started to slow down.
Ann ran on and won by two yards.
"I won! I won!" shouted Ann jumping up
   and down.

Sam sat down to eat some bread and ham.
   He took a big bite.
"I think I'll get a sweet drink," he said.
He put his bread down on the arm of the
   chair, and went to get his sweet drink.

The dog walked up to the chair
and picked up the bread. Sam
spotted him.
"Hey, put that down," shouted Sam.

The dog did not put it down.
He kept it in his mouth and ran out.
"Come back here, you bad dog," cried
    Sam.
Sam ran after the dog. The dog ran out of
    the door, holding the bread in his mouth.
    Sam ran after him. The dog ran
    down the street. Sam chased after him.

The dog ran past Sita and Mohan.
Sam ran past them too.
"Come back with my bread," he called.
The dog did not stop.
He did not come back with the bread.
The dog ran past Ann and David.
Sam kept on running. He passed Ann and
   David, too.
Now he was getting tired. He wanted to
   stop, but he wanted to catch the dog.

Just then another dog came up. He wanted
   the bread, too. He was big and strong.
He ran to Sam's dog, and growled.
Sam's dog dropped the bread and ran off.
The big dog rushed after him.

Sam picked up the bread. It was wet and
  chewed.
The other boys and girls came up to Sam.
"What happened?" they asked.
"That silly old dog took my bread and
  ham," he said. "Now look at it.
  It's no use now. What can I do with it?"
They all laughed at him.
"You can give it back to the dog," said
  David.
They all laughed again. Poor Sam!

| medal | handle | bicycle |
| pedal | saddle | |

fast	faster	fastest
slow	slower	slowest
hard	harder	hardest
soft	softer	softest
big	bigger	biggest
small	smaller	smallest

One day the boys went to town.
They looked at the toys in the shop
   windows.
They liked the sports shop and the bicycle
   shop best.
"When I get big I want a bicycle like that,"
   said David.
He pointed to a sports cycle.
It had a handle like a racing cycle,
   but there were brakes on it.
It was painted blue.

"I hope I get that one for Christmas,"
    said Mohan. He was looking at a cycle at
    the back.
It was a red racer.
"That's too big for you," said John.
    "If you sit on the saddle you will not be
    able to reach the pedals."
"That's all right," replied Mohan.
    "I don't have to sit on the saddle.
    I can sit on the bar."
You'll fall off," said John.
"Oh, no," said Mohan. "Let's go inside."

The boys went into the store.
A salesman came up to them.
"Can I help you, boys?" he asked.
"Yes," said Mohan. "Can I get on that
  bike?"
"Sure, let me help you," said the
  salesman.
He helped Mohan up. "I want to be a great
  rider and win lots of medals." He sat on
  the saddle and held on to the handlebar,
  but his feet could not reach the pedals.

"You'll have to wait a long time
   before you can ride this," said the
   salesman.
The others smiled, but Mohan was sad.
   He wanted the red racer so much.
The boys walked home slowly.
That night Mohan dreamt that he was a
   great cyclist, and won many races and
   medals.

cycle   cyclist
motor   motorist
travel   traveller
rocket

Mohan told the others about his dream.
"I want to be a famous cyclist," he said.
"I want to be famous too," said Sita.
"Me too," said John. "I want to be a pilot.
   I want to fly a big jumbo jet to all parts of
   the world.
"I want to be a space traveller," said Tim.
"I'll travel to the moon and Mars and
   Venus. I might even discover new
   worlds."

"I want to be an air hostess," said Ann.
"I'll fly in John's plane.
"We'll travel to all the big cities
of the world. Tim can go into
space with his rocket if he wants."

"All I want is a bicycle," said Mohan.
  "You want rockets and jumbo jets to go
  to the moon and the planets. You'll never
  get that."
"We know," replied Ann. "But we can
  dream too, even if we're not sleeping."

"Come on," said Sam.
"It's time for school."
"Oh yes," cried the others.
They jumped up, picked up their books,
and set off for school.

Sita sat down on the step.
She put her head in her hands
  and started to daydream.
She was an air hostess on a big plane.
She stood at the door and smiled.
  "Good morning, Sir. I hope you have a
  nice trip with us. If you need anything
  just call me and I will try to help you."

Word List

liked	excited	tried		brown	loud
looked	wanted	cried		down	proud
walked	shouted	fried		crown	cloud
talked	waited	called		crowd	round
picked	painted			fowl	mound
				howl	sound

tool	good	bark	call	corn	caught
fool	hood	dark	ball	worn	taught
cool	stood	park	fall	torn	sought
pool	look	card	hall	port	nought
school	book	hard	wall	sort	fought
stool	shook	lard	tall	sport	bought

paid	sale	bay	meet	meat
raid	tale	pay	feet	seat
afraid	tame	stay	feel	team
main	game	spray	steel	scream
rain	same	stray	sweet	stream
gain	shame	play	street	dream
		pray	judge	
			fudge	
			wedge	

like	dirt	fur	care	pole
bike	first	burn	fare	stole
line	thirst	turn	hare	lone
fine	bird	earn	stare	home
mine	third	learn	share	note
lime	girl	earl	spare	vote

cry	song	find	saddle	dawn
try	long	kind	handle	lawn
fry	strong	wind	kettle	hawk
shy	wrong	mind	pedal	awkward
reply	belong	sound		awful
supply		found		lawful
		bound		
		ground		

hard	harder	hardest
fast	faster	fastest
nice	nicer	nicest
long	longer	longest
sweet	sweeter	sweetest
soft	softer	softest

paint	painter	art	artist
build	builder	cycle	cyclist
walk	walker	organ	organist
run	runner	guitar	guitarist
play	player		
write	writer		

happy	happily
slow	slowly
sweet	sweetly
nice	nicely
quick	quickly
sad	sadly